Sink or Float?

Sheila Sweeny Higginson

Rigby
A Harcourt Achieve Imprint

www.Rigby.com
1-800-531-5015

MW01124124

Some things float.
Some things sink.
Has that ever
made you think?

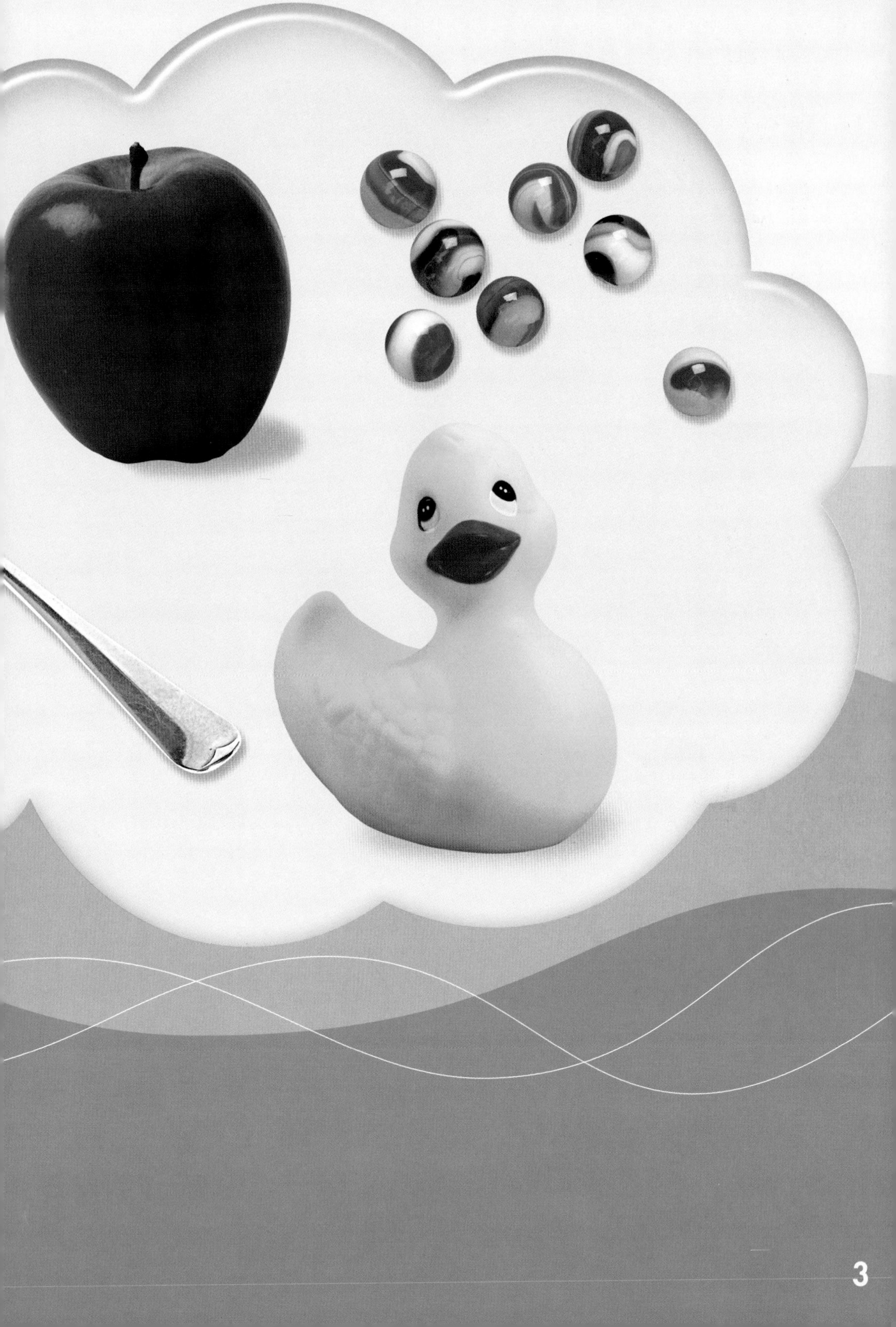

Some big things,
like this ocean boat,
sit on top of the water.
That's what it means to float.

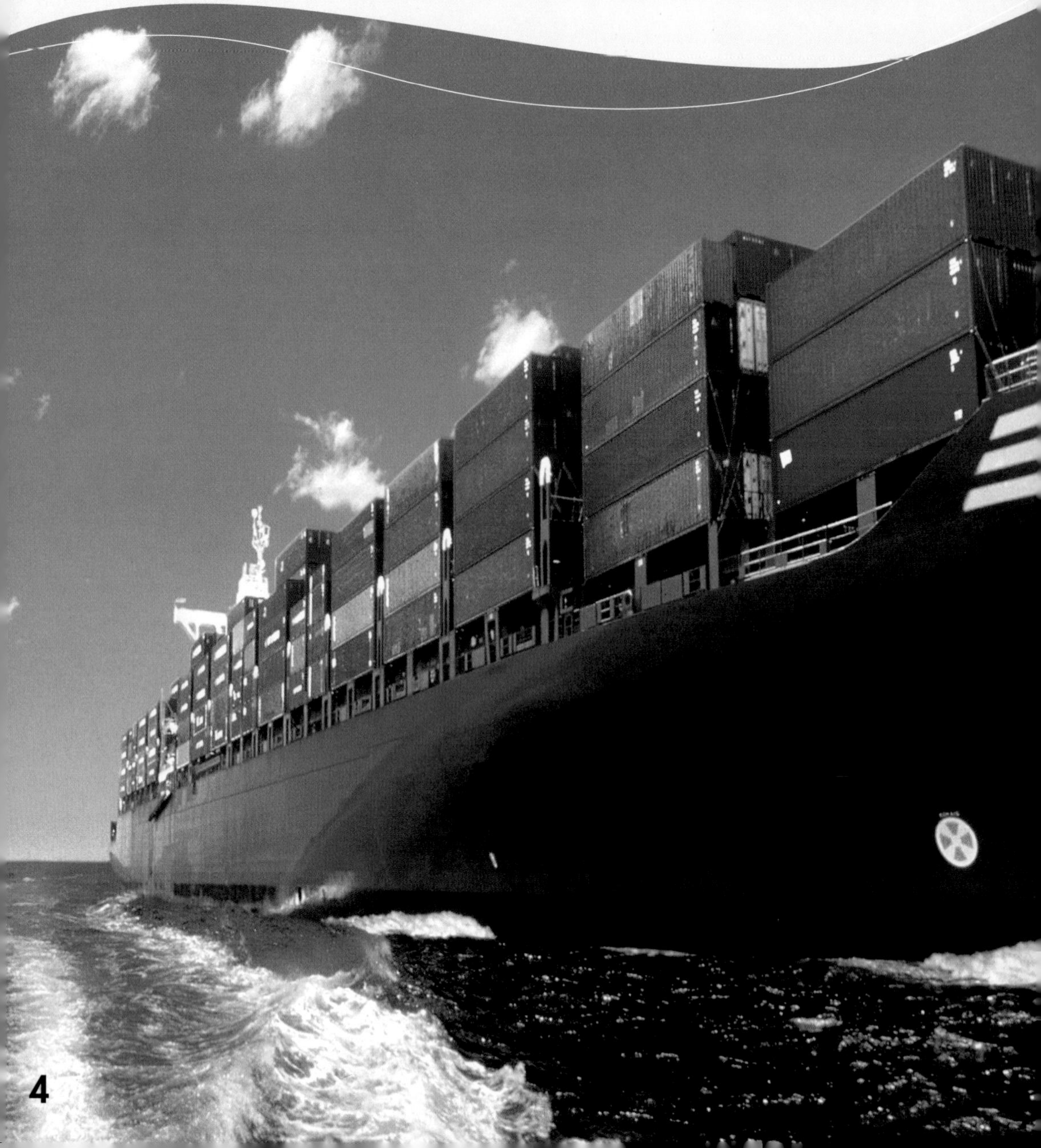

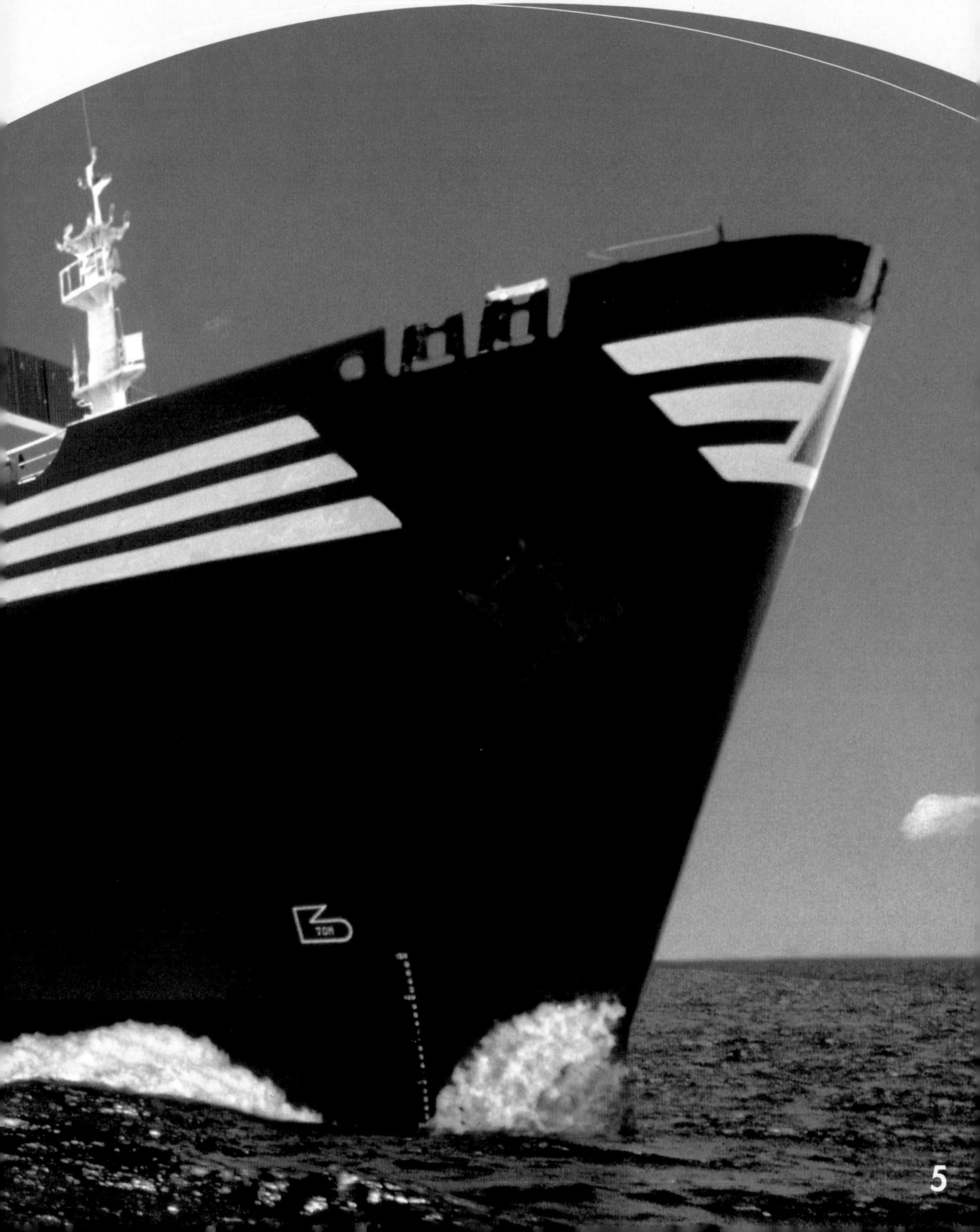

And some small things,
like these coins that clink,
fall below the water's surface.
That's what it means to sink.

We know a fun experiment.
We will show you how.
Will our things sink or float?
Let's find out now!

What You Need

✔ A bucket of water

✔ A table

✔ Paper and pencil to write down the results

Pencil

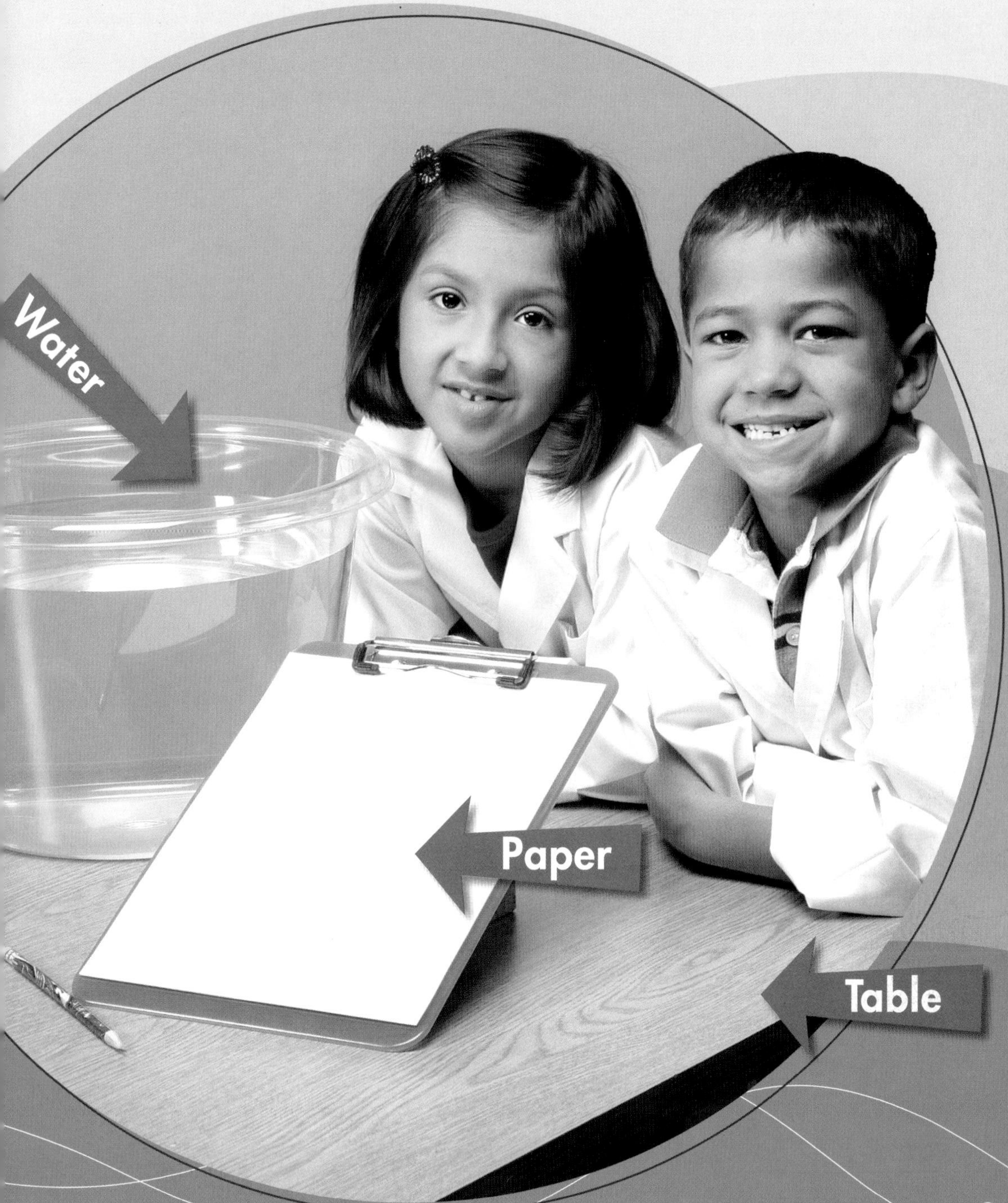
Water
Paper
Table

Step 1

Look, look,
all around,
in your pockets
and on the ground.

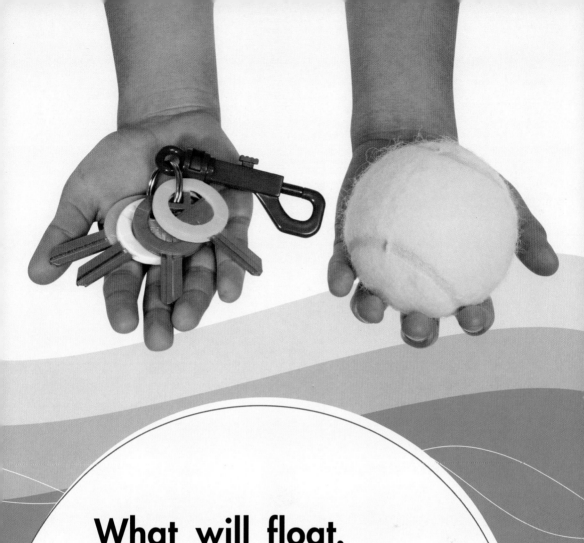

What will float,
and what will sink?
Whisper softly
what you think.

Step 2

Drop the objects into the water.

Which things float?
Which things sink?
Are you surprised?
What did you think?

Step 3
Write down your results.

Now write down
how it went.
You just did
an experiment!

Step 4
Share your results.

Tell your partner.
Tell your buddy.
What did you learn
from this study?

Results

Sink	Float
	stick
keys	
	ball
rock	

Keep looking every day
at each new thing
that comes your way.

Will it float or will it sink?
Whisper softly what you think.